Go to Joseph
for Children

Consecration to St. Joseph
for Children and Families

Go to Joseph
for Children

Consecration to St. Joseph
for Children and Families

Written by Renzo and Monica Ortega
Illustrated by The Simple Saints

TwoBecomeFamily.com
@twobecomefamily
twobecomefamily@gmail.com

TheSimpleSaints.com
@thesimplesaints
thesimplesaints@gmail.com

A Special Gift:

For complementary downloadable
coloring pages to accompany this book, visit:
twobecomefamily.com/gotojoseph
or thesimplesaints.com/gotojoseph

Go To Joseph For Children: Consecration to St. Joseph For Children and Families
by Renzo and Monica Ortega

Cover, interior design, and illustrations by The Simple Saints © Jaimee Keogler
Edited by Katie Keogler

ISBN: 978-0-578-31550-8
Published in the United States by
Two Become Family, LLC.

www.TwoBecomeFamily.com

Printed in the United States of America

DEDICATION

This book is dedicated to our children,
to our godchildren and their families,
and to the godparents of our children
and their families.

We love you and pray that
Our Lady & St. Joseph protect you always.

FROM THE AUTHORS

Dear Reader,

We are so glad you have chosen this book to help you grow closer to Jesus through learning more about St. Joseph. Our family has a special devotion to St. Joseph. He loves our family and has taken good care of us, and he loves and cares for you, too!

This book will guide you through parts of the Gospel so that you can see how St. Joseph plays a role in salvation history, in the life of Jesus, and in our lives today.

We hope that you and your family can read this together, practice virtue together, and learn to love Jesus together using the example of St. Joseph. Know that we are praying for you, through the intercession of St. Joseph.

Sincerely,

Renzo & Monica Ortega

TwoBecomeFamily.com

A NOTE TO PARENTS

We wrote this book in order to guide families as they prepare to consecrate themselves to Jesus through St. Joseph. We've included a few daily steps to learn about Joseph and reflect on his example of faith. We encourage you to adjust how you use them to the age and interest of your children.

STEP ONE

Read the Gospel verses listed from your own family Bible

STEP TWO

Reflect on the Gospel Summary for each day

STEP THREE

Think about the Saint Quote

STEP FOUR

Read the Practical Reflection

STEP FIVE

Use the Discussion Questions to prompt your own family conversation

STEP SIX

Conclude with the Go to Joseph Prayer

Also included are ten beautiful images of St. Joseph and the Holy Family to accompany your reading, discussion, and prayer time.

KEY WORDS

Here are some key words that may help you to better understand what a preparation for consecration is:

PREPARATION - a fancy word for getting ready. Preparing for this consecration means taking the steps to learn about St. Joseph to be sure that you know all about the Saint you are consecrating yourself to.

CONSECRATION - to entrust yourself to a Saint for special protection and help. In this book, you will prepare to consecrate yourself to St. Joseph. This means that you will learn how to grow closer to Jesus by following St. Joseph's example and by asking for his help and protection. Since God the Father trusted Joseph to care for and raise Jesus, we can trust Joseph to care for us and raise us, too.

INTERCESSION - praying for someone else. We believe that we can ask St. Joseph to intercede for us or pray for us. Since St. Joseph was Jesus's earthly father, we know that he continues to have a close relationship with Jesus in Heaven.

Go to Joseph for Children

Consecration to St. Joseph
for Children and Families

DAY 1

Matthew 1:1-16

GOSPEL SUMMARY

At the very beginning of his Gospel, St. Matthew shares the genealogy, or family tree, of Jesus. In it, he shows that St. Joseph's ancestors can be traced back all the way to Abraham and King David. That means that St. Joseph was related to God's chosen people of the Old Testament. He was also a blood relative of King David, meaning that St. Joseph came from a royal family! Long before St. Joseph was even born, God knew that he would be a part of the story of salvation. God had always planned for Joseph to be the foster father of Jesus.

SAINT QUOTE

"The family has the mission to guard, reveal and communicate love, and this is a living reflection of and a real sharing in God's love for humanity and the love of Christ the Lord for the Church His bride."

ST. JOHN PAUL THE GREAT

ST. JOSEPH WAS A VERY SPECIAL MAN, who was chosen for a very special mission. His mission was to be a husband to Mary and an earthly father to Jesus. As a husband and father, St. Joseph fulfilled his mission by protecting, loving, and serving his family.

GOD HAS A MISSION FOR YOU TOO! Another word for your mission is your "vocation". We all have a unique vocation, and God has given each one of us special gifts and talents so that we can fulfill our vocation. Throughout our lives, God will show us how our gifts and talents can best serve the whole world. However, the way we learn how to serve the world with our gifts is through our family.

THROUGH OUR FAMILY, God teaches us how to protect, love, and serve others. Being in a family can be difficult sometimes, but that is part of learning how to serve! Through our family, we can learn and practice forgiveness, patience, obedience, and sacrifice. It's also through our family that we are reminded that we are beloved sons and daughters of God.

DISCUSS
as a family

What mission, or vocation, do you think God is preparing you for?

When is it hardest to serve those in your family?

How can we remind each other that we are beloved sons and daughters of God?

Go To Joseph Prayer

St. Joseph, help me to love and serve my own family the way you loved and served Jesus and Mary. Teach me to use my gifts and talents to honor God and fulfill the mission that He has planned for me. Help me remember that I am a beloved son/daughter, no matter what. Help me and my family live out the mission you have called us to, by your holy example. Amen.

ST. JOSEPH, ANCESTOR OF KING DAVID
pray for us

DAY 2

Matthew 2:13-14

GOSPEL SUMMARY:

These verses tell of a time that God asked St. Joseph to act in faith to protect Jesus and Mary. He was told by an angel in a dream to flee their home and escape to Egypt because the evil King Herod wanted to harm the child Jesus. St. Joseph showed great faith by doing what he was asked to do to fulfill his mission as husband, father, and protector.

SAINT QUOTE

"The Church has commended to Joseph all of her cares, including those dangers which threaten the human family."

ST. JOHN PAUL THE GREAT

TERROR OF DEMONS

ST. JOSEPH WAS THE ONLY MAN that could fulfill the mission God gave him. He was the perfect earthly father to Jesus, the perfect husband to Mary, and the perfect protector of the Holy Family. It was St. Joseph's vocation to protect Jesus and Mary from all danger and harm. St. Joseph is still fulfilling his vocation as protector by continuing to protect us today.

WE BELIEVE THAT EVERYONE WHO IS BAPTIZED is united to Jesus as a member of the "Mystical Body of Christ." That means, through our Baptism, we are united to Jesus and are a part of His body: the Church. Since we are part of Jesus's body, St. Joseph is protecting us in the same way that he protected his son, Jesus!

WHEN WE ARE TEMPTED TO SIN, we need to go to St. Joseph. St. Joseph is ready and waiting to come protect us like a good father. Whenever you are tempted to sin, worried or nervous, or when it's hard to do the right thing, St. Joseph is ready to protect you so that you can continue on your mission.

DISCUSS
as a family

How does St. Joseph protect us like he protected Jesus?

Describe a time when it was hard to do the right thing, but you did it anyway.

Name a time when you felt worried or nervous. How can you go to St. Joseph for help next time?

Go To Joseph Prayer

St. Joseph, help me to love and serve my own family the way you loved and served Jesus and Mary. Protect me from temptation and sin. Be with me when I am worried or trying to do the right thing. Help me and my family live the mission that God has set before us even when life is difficult. Amen.

ST. JOSEPH, TERROR OF DEMONS
pray for us

DAY 3

Luke 1:26-27 & Matthew 1:20-25

GOSPEL SUMMARY – LUKE 1:26–27

St. Luke describes how the Angel Gabriel goes to Mary, who was betrothed to Joseph, to tell her of her mission from God: to be the mother of Jesus. We can imagine how scary that news must have been for Mary, but she had faith in God and in His mission for her.

MATTHEW 1:20–25

When Joseph found out Mary was pregnant with the Son of God, he was afraid. But in a dream, St. Joseph was told by the Angel Gabriel that Mary was blessed by the Holy Spirit to become the Mother of God. The Angel also told Joseph that he should take Mary into his new home like they had originally planned. Joseph woke up from his dream, and with great faith did just what the Angel had said to do.

SAINT QUOTE

"No husband and wife ever loved one another
so much as Joseph and Mary."

VENERABLE FULTON J. SHEEN

ST. JOSEPH WAS PICKED BY GOD for his mission, but that does not mean he wasn't worried about the task. St. Jerome, an expert in Scripture, teaches us that when St. Joseph learned about Mary becoming the Mother of God, he thought that he was unworthy to be the earthly father of Jesus.

ACCORDING TO ST. JEROME, Joseph was going to leave Mary quietly because he was afraid he might fail in his mission. But before St. Joseph could do that, God sent the Angel Gabriel to St. Joseph in a dream.

THE ANGEL GABRIEL REASSURED Joseph that Mary was blessed with the child Jesus through the power of the Holy Spirit. And that the Holy Spirit had chosen Joseph too! St. Joseph was reminded by Gabriel that he didn't need to have confidence in himself, but that he needed to have confidence in God. If God chose Joseph, then Joseph must be the right man for the job.

SOMETIMES OUR VOCATION seems too big or too hard for us. When we feel like our mission is too scary, we should trust God, like St. Joseph did. We must try to do our best and believe that God will do the rest.

DISCUSS
as a family

Have you ever been afraid to do something difficult? What did you do to overcome that fear?

Name two occasions that you were worried about doing well. How did they turn out in the end?

Go To Joseph Prayer

St. Joseph, help me to love and serve my own family the way you loved and served Jesus and Mary. Remind me that God has a great mission planned just for me. Help me to believe in myself and have even greater faith in God. Amen.

ST. JOSEPH, SPOUSE OF THE MOTHER OF GOD
pray for us

DAY 4

Matthew 1:20-25

GOSPEL SUMMARY

Here, St. Matthew shares the words that the Angel Gabriel spoke to St. Joseph in a dream. When Joseph found out Mary was pregnant with the Son of God, he must have been afraid. But in a dream, St. Joseph was told that Mary was blessed by the Holy Spirit to become the Mother of God, and that he should take her into his new home like they had originally planned. Joseph woke up from his dream, and with tremendous faith did just that.

SAINT QUOTE

"At the moment of Joseph's own 'annunciation' he said nothing; instead he simply 'did as the angel of the Lord commanded him.'"

ST. JOHN PAUL THE GREAT

WHEN THE ANGEL APPEARED TO ST. JOSEPH in a dream and told Joseph not to be afraid to take Mary into his home, Joseph listened to the angel's words and trusted God. He immediately did what the angel told him to do. St. Joseph shows us his faith and trust in God through his actions.

ST. JOSEPH DEMONSTRATED FAITH IN ACTION again when he had to travel with Mary to Bethlehem to complete the census even though she was pregnant. Instead of complaining to God that it was too hard, St. Joseph sprung into action.

SOMETIMES, GOD ASKS US TO DO THINGS that we don't understand. God asks us to love our enemies and to pray for those who aren't kind to us. He asks us to always do the right thing - even when it is hard to do, even when no one else is, or even when no one else will notice.

WHEN WE FOLLOW GOD'S COMMANDS by doing what God wants us to do, even if we don't fully understand why, we are putting our faith into action!

DISCUSS
as a family

How do you put your own faith into action?

How do we put our faith into action as a family?

What are three things that are hard to do, but we can choose to do anyway?

Go To Joseph Prayer

St. Joseph, help me to love and serve my own family the way you loved and served Jesus and Mary. Remind me to always do the right thing, even when it is hard, when no one else may notice, or when others may be doing the opposite. Inspire me to act when God asks and to trust in God's plan. Amen.

ST. JOSEPH, MOST OBEDIENT
pray for us

DAY 5

Matthew 2:13-14

GOSPEL SUMMARY

These verses tell of yet another time that God asked St. Joseph to act in faith to protect Jesus and Mary. This time, he was told by an angel in a dream to flee their home and escape to Egypt because the evil King Herod wanted to harm the child Jesus. And again, St. Joseph showed great faith by doing what he was asked to do to fulfill his mission as husband and father.

SAINT QUOTE

"From the example of St Joseph we all receive a strong invitation to carry out with fidelity, simplicity and modesty the task that Providence has entrusted to us."

POPE BENEDICT XVI

ST. JOSEPH SHOWS US that having faith and trusting God is not something we do only once in a while, but something we need to do all the time. After St. Joseph trusted the angel's words and took Mary into his home, he had to keep trusting. St. Joseph showed his faith and trust again as he took the Holy Family to Egypt to keep them safe from King Herod.

ST. JOSEPH'S LIFE SHOWS US that God doesn't put us in difficult situations to test our faith. God uses difficult situations to strengthen our faith. St. Joseph's faith grew with each situation, and he trusted that God would provide. He trusted that he was made for this mission.

THERE ARE TIMES WHEN HAVING FAITH in God is easy, and there are times when having faith in God is hard. St. Joseph shows us that faith is a choice to trust that God will always provide for us. If we believe that we are made for a mission, then God will help us to accomplish it.

DISCUSS
as a family

When is it easy to have faith?

When is it hard to have faith?

What is one thing we can do to grow in faith together as a family?

GO TO JOSEPH PRAYER

St. Joseph, help me to love and serve my own family the way you loved and served Jesus and Mary. When difficult moments arise, help me to be strong and have faith that God will provide. Increase my trust and faith in God's good plan for my life. Amen.

ST. JOSEPH, GUARDIAN OF THE REDEEMER
pray for us

DAY 6

Matthew 1:20-25

GOSPEL SUMMARY

In reading these verses, St. Joseph demonstrates his commitment to prayer. Because St. Joseph prayed often, he was able to hear God's message through the Angel Gabriel and respond with action.

SAINT QUOTE

"The total sacrifice, whereby Joseph surrendered his whole
existence to the demands of the Messiah's coming into
his home, becomes understandable only in the light
of his profound interior life."

ST. JOHN PAUL THE GREAT

JOSEPH MOST FAITHFUL

WHEN WE WERE BORN, we inherited original sin from Adam and Eve. At our Baptism, we were cleansed and freed from original sin, but the effects of it still remain. We feel the effects of original sin when we are tempted, when we want to do something that we know is wrong, or when we say things that we know we shouldn't. The effects of original sin make it more difficult to love God and other people the way that we should. But God has a solution for us all: His Grace.

ST. JOSEPH WAS LIKE YOU AND ME; he was born with original sin. Even still, St. Joseph was deeply devoted to God, through faith and prayer, and therefore he was able to accomplish his mission with God's Grace. St. Joseph accessed God's free gift of Grace through daily prayer.

WHEN IT IS HARD TO LOVE GOD AND OTHERS because of the effects of original sin, God provides us with His Grace to give us the strength to be holy, if we ask Him. St. Joseph asked God for His Grace every day and he was able to be the holiest husband and father. He was able to do that by God's Grace, and we can be holy with God's Grace as well!

DISCUSS
as a family

How do we experience God's Grace every day?

What Sacraments do we participate in to receive more Grace?

How can we pray for one another?

Go To Joseph Prayer

St. Joseph, help me to love and serve my own family the way you loved and served Jesus and Mary. Guide me as I prepare for my mission. Show me how to pray for and accept God's gift of Grace. Remind me to use the gift of Grace to do what is right. Help my parents to live out the mission you have called them to, by your holy example. Amen.

ST. JOSEPH, MOST FAITHFUL
pray for us

DAY 7

Matthew 2:13-14

GOSPEL SUMMARY

These verses tell us of the time St. Joseph escaped to Egypt with Jesus and Mary. This was a scary time for the Holy Family and it is St. Joseph's virtue that helped him fulfill his mission as husband and father even when it was hard.

SAINT QUOTE

"St. Joseph is the model of those humble ones that Christianity raises up to great destinies; ...he is the proof that in order to be a good and genuine follower of Christ, there is no need of great things - it is enough to have the common, simple and human virtues, but they need to be true and authentic."

POPE ST. PAUL VI

MODEL OF VIRTUE

WHEN WE SAY THAT ST. JOSEPH WAS HOLY, that does not mean that St. Joseph was perfect. On the outside, Joseph was like everyone else: he worked hard, loved his family, and tried his very best to follow God's commandments. But on the inside, St. Joseph was extraordinary because he practiced something special called "virtue".

A VIRTUE IS AN ATTITUDE, HABIT, AND WAY OF THINKING that helps us to do good, and to follow God's will. Virtues do not come easily. They take a lot of practice and a lot of Grace! We can practice growing in virtue by doing our chores the first time we're asked, waiting our turn, eating only one dessert when we want two, trying new things even if we are afraid, and by praying to God to help us grow in virtue!

ST. JOSEPH EXERCISED VIRTUE PERFECTLY, and because of that, he was able to love Jesus and Mary perfectly. That does not mean that it was easy. Having virtue does not mean that hard things will be easy. Having virtue means that you will be able to do the right things, even when they're hard.

DISCUSS
as a family

What is something good that you do not always want to do, but you do it anyway?

What are two ways that you can practice virtue?

What is one way that we can grow in virtue together as a family?

GO TO JOSEPH PRAYER

St. Joseph, help me to love and serve my own family the way you loved and served Jesus and Mary. Support me as I practice growing in virtue. Thank you for showing me that being virtuous is doing the right thing, even when it is hard. As I practice loving others well through my actions, pray for me and guide me. Amen.

ST. JOSEPH, MODEL OF VIRTUE
pray for us

DAY 8

Matthew 3:13-17

GOSPEL SUMMARY

Near the beginning of Christ's public ministry of preaching and performing miracles, He was baptized by St. John the Baptist. This is the first time that we see God the Father, God the Son, and God the Holy Spirit present in the same place. Before this display of perfect Love, we know that Jesus was also part of the perfect love of the Holy Family. It was the love of the Holy Family that prepared Jesus for His mission.

SAINT QUOTE

"God placed St. Joseph at the head of his family,
as a faithful and prudent servant, so that with fatherly care
he might watch over His only begotten Son."

ST. JOHN PAUL THE GREAT

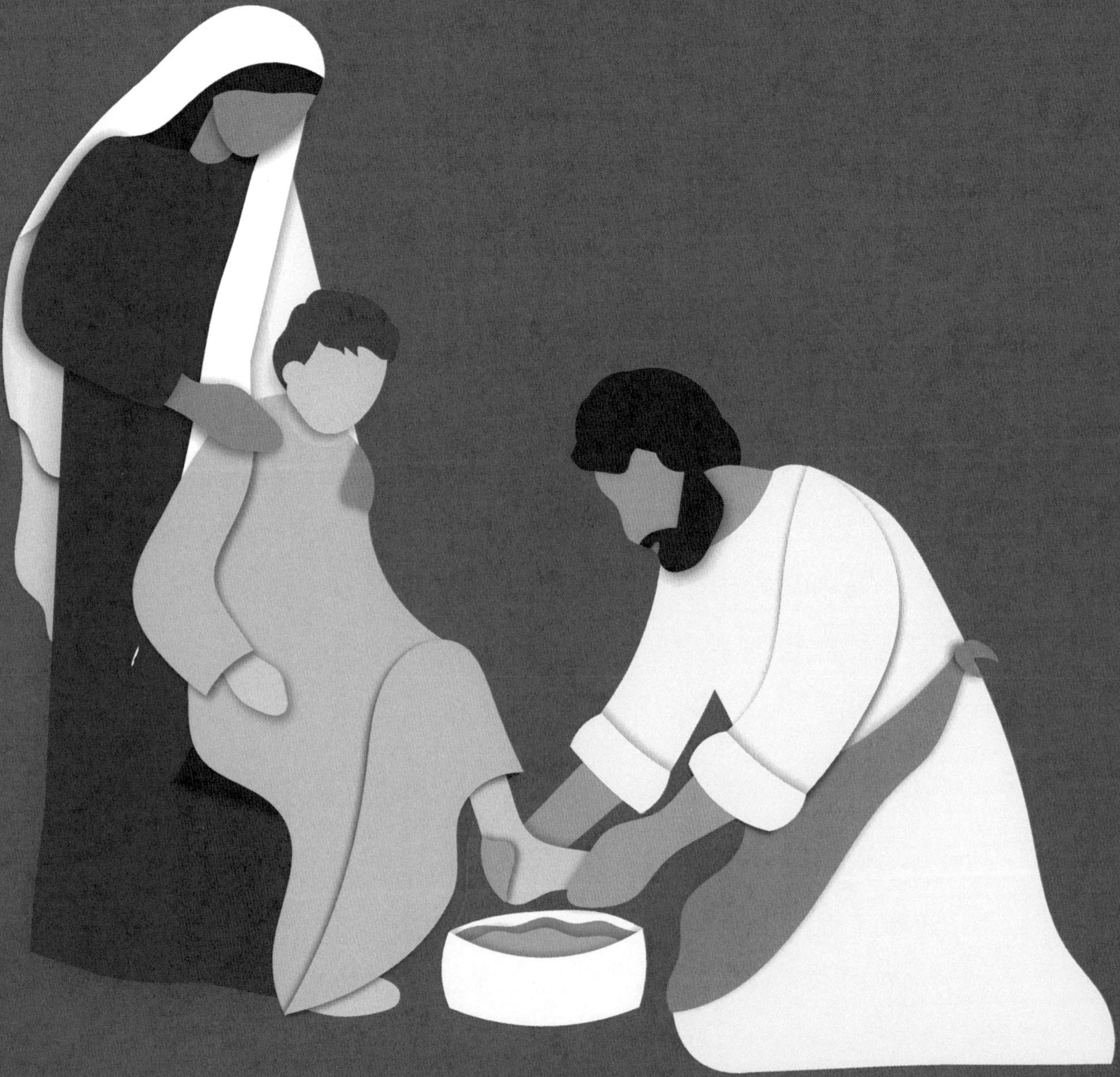

THE HOLY FAMILY is an earthly reflection of the Holy Trinity. In the Holy Trinity, God the Father loves God the Son completely. God the Son loves God the Father completely. The total and complete love between God the Father and God the Son is God the Holy Spirit. The Trinity is a perfect relationship of Love. That is why we say that God is Love!

LIKE THE HOLY TRINITY, THE HOLY FAMILY (Jesus, Mary, and St. Joseph) loved one another completely and perfectly. Jesus loved His parents and honored them like a good son. Mary loved Jesus and St. Joseph, and served them like a good mother and a good wife. St. Joseph loved Jesus and Mary and served them like a good father and a good husband.

AS THE FATHER, ST. JOSEPH WAS THE LEADER of the Holy Family. St. Joseph led his family by serving them! Serving one another means putting the needs of our family members first and our desires second. We can ask St. Joseph to show us how to love our family well by modeling his example of service.

DISCUSS
as a family

How does serving others show them that you love them?

Who are the people that your family can serve?

What is one way you serve members of your family?

GO TO JOSEPH PRAYER

St. Joseph, help me to love and serve my own family the way you loved and served Jesus and Mary. Remind me to put their needs before my own desires. Help me to think of them often and to show my love for them through my actions. Amen.

ST. JOSEPH, HEAD OF THE HOLY FAMILY
pray for us

DAY 9

Matthew 13:55

GOSPEL SUMMARY

In this selection from the Gospel of Matthew, Jesus is referred to as the son of a carpenter. The phrase was meant to identify St. Joseph by his common job: artisan, woodworker, or builder. They only knew St. Joseph as a carpenter, but we know him as a great Saint!

SAINT QUOTE

"[The Church] proclaimed the great supernatural value of St Joseph's life, the value of an ordinary life of work done in God's presence and in total fulfillment of his will."

ST. JOSEMARIA ESCRIVA

WE HAVE ALL BEEN BORN WITH A DESIRE TO BE GREAT. Some of us might want to be famous singers, authors, athletes, or even great Saints! We might want to go on daring adventures, do exciting things, and make a difference in the world. It is good that we all want to be extraordinary, because God wants us to be extraordinary too!

ST. JOSEPH'S LIFE SHOWS US that sometimes being extraordinary to God looks ordinary to the world. St. Joseph was known only as a carpenter by his friends and neighbors. For St. Joseph, being extraordinary meant going to work everyday, working hard, and loving his family as best as he could.

ST. JOSEPH LIVED AN EXTRAORDINARY LIFE by going to work and simply being the best husband and father he could be. The world remembers him as a carpenter, but we remember him as St. Joseph the Patron of the Universal Catholic Church! St. Joseph shows us that working hard and loving your family well is one of the most extraordinary things we can do for God!

DISCUSS
as a family

What are two ordinary things that you do that can become extraordinary when they are done for God?

Who is someone that seems ordinary to the world, but is extraordinary to God?

GO TO JOSEPH PRAYER

St. Joseph, help me to love and serve my own family the way you loved and served Jesus and Mary. Show me that by living my ordinary life well, I am doing extraordinary things for God and for my family. When I am tempted to think that my love and virtue are not enough, remind me that they are a part of my extraordinary mission. Amen.

ST. JOSEPH, PATRON OF THE UNIVERSAL CHURCH
pray for us

DAY 10

Matthew 13:55

GOSPEL SUMMARY

Not only does this gospel show us that an ordinary life can be extraordinary for God, but it also demonstrates the holiness of hard work. Being a carpenter took great skill and strength. St. Joseph is a great example of how work is actually an expression of love, and can be used to glorify God.

SAINT QUOTE

"Work was the daily expression of love
in the life of the Family of Nazareth."

ST. JOHN PAUL THE GREAT

ST. JOSEPH THE WORKER

LIVING A HOLY LIFE IS HARD WORK. When we live a life of holiness, that means that our bodies, our minds, and our souls are used to glorify God. When we use our bodies and minds, we glorify God by completing our responsibilities well. When we recite the rosary, go to Mass, and pray with our family, we glorify God by uniting our souls to Him.St. Joseph shows us that both our work and our prayers are important!

ST. JOSEPH LOVED GOD through both his prayers and his work as a carpenter. Just like St. Joseph, you are called to love God through your work. That might be your schoolwork, sports, hobbies, chores, or playing with others. Doing those things with a positive attitude and doing them well glorifies God.

SOMETIMES WORK IS FUN, and sometimes it's boring or difficult. Either way, it's important to work hard because it makes us stronger and better prepares us for our mission. Work hard, like St. Joseph, and ask him to teach you how to love Jesus, Mary, and your family well.

DISCUSS
as a family

What are some things that are hard work for you?

What is one way someone in your family works hard for you?

How can hard work make you more like St. Joseph?

Go To Joseph Prayer

St. Joseph, help me to love and serve my own family the way you loved and served Jesus and Mary. Thank you for showing me the value of hard work. Remind me that I can accomplish God's mission for my life by working hard in all that I do. Amen.

ST. JOSEPH, THE WORKER
pray for us

"Go to Joseph.
Get to know Joseph and you will find Jesus.
Talk to Joseph and you will find Mary."

ST. JOSEMARIA ESCRIVA

CONSECRATION DAY

congratulations!

You and your family are ready
to consecrate yourselves to St. Joseph!

STEP ONE

Go to Mass together

STEP TWO

After Mass, pray the Family Consecration Prayer

STEP THREE

Pray the Daily Consecration Prayer every day

Free printable versions of these prayers are available for download at:
www.twobecomefamily.com/gotojoseph
www.thesimplesaints.com/gotojoseph

FAMILY CONSECRATION
prayer

St. Joseph, I consecrate and entrust myself
and my family to your loving protection.
Help me to love and serve my own family
the way you loved and served Jesus and Mary.
Remind me that God has a great mission planned just for me, and that I
can accomplish God's mission for my life by working hard in all that I do.
Inspire me to act when God asks and to trust in God's plan.
Teach me to use my gifts and talents to honor God
and fulfill the mission that He has planned for me.
Show me that by living my ordinary life well,
I am doing extraordinary things for God.
Protect me from temptation and sin.
Be with me when I am worried or trying to do the right thing.
Support me as I practice growing in virtue, even when it is hard.
Help me remember that I am a beloved son/daughter no matter what.
Help me and my family live out the mission God has called us to,
by your holy example.

amen

DAILY CONSECRATION
prayer

Jesus, I offer my life to you.
Mary, I honor you.
St. Joseph, I consecrate myself to you.

amen

PRAYER OF ST. JOHN PAUL THE GREAT
for families

Lord God, from You every family
in Heaven and on earth takes its name.
Father, You are love and life.

Through Your Son, Jesus Christ, born of woman, and through the Holy Spirit, the fountain of divine charity, grant that every family on earth may become for each successive generation a true shrine of life and love.

Grant that Your grace may guide the thoughts and actions of husbands and wives for the good of their families and of all the families in the world.

Grant that the young may find in the family solid support for their human dignity and for their growth in truth and love.
Grant that love, strengthened by the grace of the sacrament of marriage, may prove mightier than all the weaknesses and trials through which our families sometimes pass.

Through the intercession of the Holy Family of Nazareth, grant that the Church may fruitfully carry out her worldwide mission in the family and through the family.

We ask this of You, Who is life, truth and love
with the Son and the Holy Spirit.

amen

MORE ABOUT
The Authors

Renzo and Monica Ortega are high school youth ministers and young adult mentors. They have coordinated and facilitated Marriage Formation Programs for the Diocese of Bridgeport, and volunteer as a mentor couple at the Pre-Cana retreats at their home parish. They live in Connecticut with their five children.

MORE ABOUT
Two Become Family

At Two Become Family, our goal is to restore confidence in family life again. St. John Paul the Great accurately portrays the state of many families today when he said, "The modern Christian family is often tempted to be discouraged and is distressed at the growth of its difficulties." There are so many difficulties that families face. You would be hard-pressed to find a family, including ours, that would claim that they did not experience any difficulties while navigating family life.

The mission is not to tell families to follow our example in order to find peace. Our goal is to encourage the family to have, "confidence in itself, in the riches that it possesses by nature and grace, and in the mission that God has entrusted to it." (Familiaris Consortio)

Every Catholic family possesses all that it needs to succeed, by nature and by grace. In the midst of difficulties and hardships, families need not look beyond the Sacrament that binds them. Our articles, videos, social media posts, and books are directed towards that end. We want to give families confidence that they have what it takes.

YOU HAVE WHAT IT TAKES TO HAVE AN AMAZING MARRIAGE, TO RAISE BEAUTIFUL CHILDREN, AND TO SERVE CHRIST AND HIS CHURCH THROUGH YOUR FAMILY!

MORE ABOUT
The Simple Saints

Surround yourself with a great cloud of witnesses!
The Simple Saints provide subtle, beautiful, simplified images of your favorite Catholic Saints.

Find out more by visiting:
TheSimpleSaints.com
and by following:
@thesimplesaints

Made in the USA
Coppell, TX
17 March 2023

14360455R00038